CONTENTS

INTERACTIONS

In 1992, Willow Creek Community Church, in partnership with Zondervan and the Willow Creek Association, released a curriculum for small groups entitled the Walking with God series. In just three years, almost a half million copies of these small group study guides were being used in churches around the world. The phenomenal response to this curriculum affirmed the need for relevant and biblical small group materials.

At the writing of this curriculum, there are nearly three 3,000 small groups meeting regularly within the structure of Willow Creek Community Church. We believe this number will increase as we continue to place a central value on small groups. Many other churches throughout the world are growing in their commitment to small group ministries as well, so the need for resources is increasing.

In response to this great need, the Interactions small group series has been developed. Willow Creek Association and Zondervan have joined together to create a whole new approach to small group materials. These discussion guides are meant to challenge group members to a deeper level of sharing, to create lines of accountability, to move followers of Christ into action, and to help group members become fully devoted followers of Christ.

SUGGESTIONS FOR INDIVIDUAL STUDY

1. Begin each session with prayer. Ask God to help you understand the passage and to apply it to your life.
2. A good modern translation, such as the New International Version, the New American Standard Bible, or the New Revised Standard Version, will give you the most help. Questions in this guide are based on the New International Version.
3. Read and reread the passage(s). You must know what the passage says before you can undersand what it means and how it applies to you.
4. Write your answers in the spaces provided in the study guide. This will help you to express clearly your understanding of the passage.

5. Keep a Bible dictionary handy. Use it to look up unfamiliar words, names, or places.

SUGGESTIONS FOR GROUP STUDY

1. Come to the session prepared. Careful preparation will greatly enrich your time in group discussion.
2. Be willing to join in the discussion. The leader of the group will not be lecturing, but will encourage people to discuss what they have learned in the passage. Plan to share what God has taught you in your individual study.
3. Stick to the passage being studied. Base your answers on the verses being discussed rather than on outside authorities such as commentaries or your favorite author or speaker.
4. Try to be sensitive to the other members of the group. Listen attentively when they speak, and be affirming whenever you can. This will encourage more hesitant members of the group to participate.
5. Be careful not to dominate the discussion. By all means participate, but allow others to have equal time.
6. If you are the discussion leader, you will find additional suggestions and helpful ideas in the Leader's Notes.

ADDITIONAL RESOURCES AND TEACHING MATERIALS

At the end of this study guide you will find a collection of resources and teaching materials to help you in your growth as a follower of Christ. You will also find resources that will help your church develop and build fully devoted followers of Christ.

Introduction: Living the Supernatural Life

I face a hard reality every day of my life: I have a war going on inside of me. It's been going on for a long, long time, and it causes me a considerable amount of anguish. Sometimes I feel like I'm winning the war and have the enemy on the run. And then there are times when I feel like I am retreating as fast as I can, wounded and losing the battle. In fact, during those times I feel like I'm being overrun and overwhelmed by the opposition.

You might wonder who I am fighting. To be honest, I'm fighting everyone! I'm fighting my wife and kids, church board members, elders, staff members, neighbors, the butcher, the baker, the candlestick maker. Sometimes it seems like I'm at war with everyone in my life.

The war raging inside of me pretty much stems from a principle in Scripture found throughout the Bible, but crystallized clearly in Philippians 2:3. It simply says, "Do nothing out of selfish ambition or vain conceit, but *in humility consider others better than yourselves.*" Those final seven words in this verse have set off the war: I am to treat other people as though they are more important than myself.

I would have no trouble treating a real celebrity as more important than myself. I would have little trouble treating a very important person courteously, graciously, and with great respect. If I were informed that the president, a world leader, or royalty was coming to the Hybel's house for dinner, I would be a model host. There would be no question how I would treat him or her. I would open car doors, front doors, and closet doors. I would listen intently to every word spoken, laugh at anything bordering humorous, offer the best seat at the head of the table. My esteemed visitor would be served first, given the most generous portion of our dessert, escorted to the limo, and be waved to as the motorcade left my street. There would not be a war going on inside of me if I were asked to treat a bona fide VIP as more important than myself.

The war begins when I realize I am called to treat everyone with this same level of care and dignity. The rubber hits the road when I realize I should treat my wife as more important than myself. You see, when she comes home for dinner, she drives her own car, opens her own doors, and takes care of her own coat. More than likely, I will not be as attentive to her conversation as I should be, and I might even get a little irritated with her if she puts any demands on me after my hard day of work. You see, because she's "just" my wife, when I'm not very, very careful, I begin to think that I'm more important than she is. I hate to admit it, but it's true.

I would imagine, when you are honest with yourself, that you sometimes feel the same way. Our human tendency is not to treat others as better than ourselves, but to put ourselves first. However, God calls us to have our whole perspective on life transformed by His supernatural power.

How does this happen?

It happens when we are filled with the supernatural power of the Holy Spirit. As He works in our hearts and His fruit grows in our lives, we see things change. We begin to learn how to treat others with love and dignity. We become patient and gentle. We find strength we never knew existed. We see people differently. That goes for the gas station attendant, the mailman, the towel man at the YMCA, and the kid that delivers the paper. This is a tall order for self-centered human beings because our natural instinct tends to say, "I am the most important person in my world."

In short, as we learn to live the supernatural life, we learn to treat common people like VIPs. This is what God is doing in my life. I am learning to put my wife and kids' interests, the church's interests, the staff's interests, and my friends' interests *before* my own.

In these six sessions we're going to learn about love, joy, peace, patience, sensitivity, and faithfulness. It is my desire that these sessions will give you the key to unlocking the door to the supernatural life that will transform every relationship you have. The good news is that if you are willing to enter the war to build your character, reinforcements are already in place. The Holy Spirit is just waiting to supernaturally give you the ability to develop the kind of character that bears the fruit of the Spirit.

> But the fruit of the Spirit is love, joy, peace, patience, kindness, goodness, faithfulness, gentleness and self-control. Against such things there is no law. Those who belong to Christ Jesus have crucified the sinful nature with its passions and desires. Since we live by the Spirit, let us keep in step with the Spirit.
>
> *Galatians 5:22–25*

Bill Hybels

LOVE

THE BIG PICTURE

It takes an enormous amount of courage to enter the character battles that Scripture challenges us to fight. I would like to propose that *treating others as more important than yourself* is one of the best definitions of love I have ever heard. I get so tired of superficial definitions of love. They seem to change with the seasons.

- Love is a gentle smile.
- Love is finding someone's space that is similar to your own.
- Love is standing up in a church service and shaking hands with people.
- Love is feeling warm and sentimental toward other believers.
- Love is the feeling you get when you are near someone attractive.

This is all lightweight, hollow stuff. The Bible cuts through all of the haze and says that if you want one clear definition of what love is, treat every person as though they were more important than you. This means you should treat family members, friends, employees, minorities, Republicans, and Democrats as though they are more important than you are. It means you should learn to honor others. To hold them in high esteem. To respect them. To believe they have something to contribute to your life.

A WIDE ANGLE VIEW

1 How would you have defined love at *one* of the following times in your life:

- When you were a child
- When you were a teenager
- When you were a young adult

How has your understanding of love changed over the years?

Perseverance ; respect

A BIBLICAL PORTRAIT

Read Philippians 2:1–11

2 What does this passage teach about what love looks like?

(Taoism)

Empty yourself of yourself, & putting others first.

3 What has Jesus done to model perfect love for us?

How can we follow Jesus' example of love? *Love others.*
Do the action, just don't think
about it.

SHARPENING THE FOCUS

Read Snapshot "Putting Others First, Even at One O'clock in the Morning"

PUTTING OTHERS FIRST, EVEN AT ONE O'CLOCK IN THE MORNING

I remember an experience some years ago when I was awakened at about 1:00 A.M. by our son, Todd, then five years old, who said, "Mom. Dad. I just had a nightmare." As soon as I awakened, my instinct was to lay very still and pretend I was asleep so Lynne would get up and deal with him. After he kept trying to get our attention, I poked her and said, "Lynne, Todd had a nightmare." I was hoping she would be so startled that her motherly instincts would take over. It worked like a charm. She jumped up and took care of him. But as I lay there, trying to doze off to sleep, I found myself thinking, "Oh no! This was a great opportunity to treat my wife as more important than myself, and all I could think of was me."

---

4 Tell your small group about a time you had a chance to treat someone else as better than yourself but failed to do so. *Mary & Pat*

Tell about a time you received God's supernatural power and were able to love another person by treating him or her as better than yourself.

Read Snapshot "The Power of the Spirit"

THE POWER OF THE SPIRIT

The primary means by which God accomplishes His transformation in our lives is through the work of His Holy Spirit. If you have surrendered your life to Christ and asked Him to be your Savior and friend, one of the first things God does is put His Holy Spirit, the third person of the Trinity, into your life. Through the Spirit, He begins the process of transformation. He begins to work twenty-four hours a day to change your natural instincts so that you begin to act and react to people in a supernatural, God-honoring fashion. The Holy Spirit will always be faithful to grow this kind of love in your life. The big question is, will you cooperate?

5 How have you experienced the transforming power and presence of the Holy Spirit in your life since becoming a follower of Christ?

6 Describe a time when you did not fully cooperate with the Spirit's work or prompting. What were the consequences?

Read Snapshot "God's Example of Love"

GOD'S EXAMPLE OF LOVE

Our God is wonderful, amazing, and loving beyond our understanding. He treats us like celebrities. We are VIPs in His sight. He even put our needs and interests above His own by giving His only Son for us. What greater motivation could we have to love others?

7

Choose one area below and list a practical way you can show love by putting the needs of others ahead of your own needs.

- Your home
- Your workplace — be patient c̄ others ar B FAIR
- Your neighborhood
- Your small group
- Your church
- Your community

What can your small group members do to support you and keep you accountable as you seek to express love in this area?

prayer

8

Describe a recurring situation in your life where putting others first is difficult.

Taking care of my parents.

What is one thing you can do to begin to change in this area of your life?

Slow down; "be gentle"

15

PUTTING YOURSELF IN THE PICTURE

PUTTING OTHERS FIRST

Take time in the coming week to identify one person you
need to love by putting that person's interests and needs
before your own. Decide exactly how you will express love to
that person by putting him or her first.

To whom will you be expressing love?

What will you do to put that person first?

When will you do it?

Who will be praying for you and keeping you accountable?

HOW WILL YOU BE REMEMBERED?

I remember attending the funeral of a man from our church
some years ago. One of the things said about him during the
eulogy was, "He put others first." All the way through that
funeral, the Spirit put a mirror of reflection in front of me
which caused me to wonder, "What are they going to say
about me at my funeral? He was intense? He was a leader?" I
hope people will say, "He loved others. He put others first."

Take time for honest and prayerful reflection and answer the
following questions:

If you were to die today, what do you think people would say
about you and the impact your life has made? What would
you like people to say about you after you are gone?

JOY

REFLECTIONS FROM SESSION 1

1. If you specifically showed God's love by putting someone else first, tell how this person responded to you.
   Describe how it felt to put someone else's needs and
   interests before your own.
2. If you wrote a statement of what you would hope others
   would say about you after you die, would you be willing
   to read this statement to the group? What are you doing
   now to make this hope a reality?

THE BIG PICTURE

It's not very often that I feel the freedom or the confidence to
make a sweeping, categorical statement, but I think I can
make one about the topic of this study. I have the confidence
to say that every single person reading these words would
rather be happy than sad.

If you were given a choice, I think you would choose gladness
over sadness. I am confident you would rather be up than
down. I'm pretty sure you would rather attend a wedding, a
birthday party, or a graduation than a funeral. You would
rather dance, sing, and shout than mourn, grieve, and weep.
Many absolute statements seem to have exceptions, but I can
pretty safely say that all of us prefer joy to sadness.

I might even go a step further and say that most of us prefer to
be around those who are joyful. In moments of truthful con-
templation, I have to admit that sometimes I choose friends
on the basis of their joy quotient. I like to be around positive
people. Sometimes I even find myself avoiding individuals
who are always down. I know that God calls me to minister
to all people regardless of their predominant mood, and to try
to lift them up, but if I have a free Saturday afternoon and I
want to spend some time with somebody, chances are I'll lean
toward a person who is filled with joy.

I also believe many people choose churches on the basis of whether or not they find a sense of joy, celebration, and excitement there. Is your church more positive than negative? More joyful than sorrowful? We all have a natural hunger for that which lifts us up and brings us joy.

A WIDE ANGLE VIEW

1 What brings you joy and happiness?

enjoying themselves (i.e. Fun Club a happy moments at BPAIR. Seeing disabled people really

What takes away your joy and happiness?

A BIBLICAL PORTRAIT

Read John 15:9–11

2 Jesus talks about our joy being "complete." How was your joy *incomplete* before Jesus entered your life?

3 Jesus said, "I have told you this so that *my joy may be in you . . .*" What is unique about the joy Jesus brings us?

What has God done to bring you joy over the past year?

> Enabled Fan Club to develop & grow in #'s
> Given me the opportunity to work at BPAJR where I
> can & work independently with the individuals. 5
> being told what to do!)

SHARPENING THE FOCUS

Read Snapshot "The Armchair Experts"

THE ARMCHAIR EXPERTS

Armchair experts are those people who offer free advice for anything that ails you. We can all remember a time when we had the "blues" and a friend, family member, or acquaintance detected our condition. As soon as they realized we were down, the advice started flowing from these armchair experts. They said things like, "Well, I'll tell you what. Let's just go out and get drunk tonight and then you'll feel better." Or "Just snap out of it! That's all you gotta do. Get over it!" Or maybe they said, "What you need is a break. Go home and take a nap and you'll feel better." They usually mean well, but their advice seems hollow and it rarely brings joy to a joyless heart.

4 How did you feel when an armchair expert offered advice to you?

How did it go when you followed that person's advice?

Read Snapshot "The Psychological Experts"

THE PSYCHOLOGICAL EXPERTS

Over the years, another group of people have been researching the problem of the "blues." They have gone about their research in a thoroughly professional fashion. Some of them are extremely bright, insightful, and sensitive. Many of them have spent decades studying the dilemma of the absence of joy in the human heart. These psychological experts have come to conclusions concerning joy and happiness, some of which are worth pondering. Here are very brief summaries on the findings of three such experts:

- *William Glasser:* Joy and happiness are found when we have *significant love relationships* in our lives.
- *Viktor Frankl:* Joy comes when we have *meaning in life* and a purpose for living.
- *Bruno Bettelheim:* Joy comes when we *live with hope*, something to look forward to.

5 How do these experts capture some of the meaning of joy?

How do these definitions fall short of the full meaning of joy?

Read Snapshot "A Biblical Perspective"

A BIBLICAL PERSPECTIVE

I want to focus on two great biblical truths pertaining to personal joy and happiness. Here's the first one: God loves you so much that He makes it a priority to produce a spirit of joy in your life. He has committed Himself to growing joy within you through the supernatural power of His Spirit. He wants to produce a joy so deep in your life that it will transcend any pain, discouragement, and circumstantial problems you have.

A second great truth, connected to the first, is that our God has a brilliant plan for carrying out His objective. His plan is to first fill your life with significant love relationships. Then He's going to give your life a purpose—an eternal significance. And finally, He is going to instill a hope in your life that will last for eternity.

6

How has your relationship with God brought you significant love relationships?

Write down the names of four people God has brought into your life who express a deep, Christlike love for you:

- Kathy Thompson
- Gail D.
- Doug
- Sam

Tell your group members how one of these people has brought joy to your life.

7

How has your relationship with Christ given you meaning in life?

8 How does your walk with Christ provide hope both now and for your eternity?

How does this hope increase your joy?

PUTTING YOURSELF IN THE PICTURE

PRAISE FOR PEOPLE

God has placed us into a community with other followers of Christ, and these relationships are intended to bring us great joy. Take time in the coming week to write a note to one person who, through loving you with God's love, has brought joy to your life. Thank the person very specifically for how they have impacted your life with their love.

REJOICING IN HOPE

Hope produces joy in our hearts. As followers of Christ, we live with hope for today, for the years ahead, and for eternity.

SESSION 3   FRUIT OF THE SPIRIT

PEACE

REFLECTIONS FROM SESSION 2

1. If you took time to write a note to someone expressing thankfulness for how God has used them to bring joy in your life, how did this action increase your joy?
2. If you have been taking time to reflect on the hope you have in Christ, how has this increased your joy?

THE BIG PICTURE

If you went to a war-torn part of the world and asked for a definition of peace, chances are someone would stare at you with glazed, bloodshot eyes and say peace means laying the weapons down, sending the troops home, and putting the rifles back in their racks. They might even say, "What else could peace mean? Isn't it obvious? *Peace means the end of hostilities.*" We all have a sense that peace is about an absence of conflict and hostility. I call this definition of peace "P_1" peace. P_1 peace is the end (or absence) of hostility, conflict, and fighting.

In the world, we all long for P_1 peace. No one wants to live in conflict-filled, war-torn relationships. However, this is not the whole picture of peace. Jesus says that He wants to give us an even deeper kind of peace that can only come through His supernatural power and the working of the Holy Spirit. This is what I call "P_2" peace. P_2 peace is the peace of God that not only takes away conflict, but goes a step further. God's P_2 peace heals relationships, brings us into intimate friendship, and gives us a new beginning in our relationships. This is the peace we all hunger for in the deepest part of our hearts.

A WIDE ANGLE VIEW

1 What does peace look like when it's fleshed out? Choose _one_ area below and describe what it would mean to have peace there.

- In a family
- In a neighborhood
- In a church
- In a nation

A BIBLICAL PORTRAIT

Read John 14:25–27; Romans 5:1–2

2 How does God's peace differ from the peace we find in this world?

How have you experienced turmoil, conflict, and a lack of peace in this world?

Isaiah 26:3

1 Cor. 10:31

How have you experienced the peace that comes from a vital relationship with Christ?

Romans 8:28
James 1:3

3 In Romans 5:1–2, we are told that we have peace with God through Jesus Christ. How did you view God before you met Christ?

What changes did a relationship with Christ bring?

SHARPENING THE FOCUS

Read Snapshot "Peace with God"

PEACE WITH GOD

We all know people who avoid church and stay away from anything having to do with God. If you were to ask them, "Are you angry and hostile toward God?" they'd say something like, "No, I'm not. As a matter of fact, I am at peace with God." The peace they are referring to is P_1 peace. They have an arrangement: God is doing His thing, and they are doing their thing. There is no open conflict, but this is certainly not a healthy and growing relationship.

But God says, "I'm going to take it upon myself to do whatever it takes to produce P_2 peace with you. I'm going to get up close to you and break down those walls. I'm going to draw close to you and put My Holy Spirit in your life. And, for the first time in your life, you are going to find yourself attracted to Me. We are going to have a loving and healthy relationship."

Here is the truth of the matter: You and I will never find permanent peace in the center of our soul until we are in a relationship with Jesus Christ. Only by confessing our sins, by asking Christ to be our forgiver, friend, and leader of our life can we discover P_2 peace.

---

4 What does a person's life look like when he or she has only P_1 peace with God?

How does their life change when they find P_2 peace?

5 If someone asked you, "How can I have P_2 peace with God? how would you reply?

*A closer relationship thru
studying the Bible; talking & being ī other
Christians.*

Describe when you first experienced P_2 peace with God.

*When I needed His constant Love & support
in helping me ī Aidan & when in 2005 He sent
all those special believing Angels to help at
Children's & at BMC (Sean R.N.)*

Read Snapshot "Peace with Ourselves"

PEACE WITH OURSELVES

Some people believe P_2 peace is just for our relationship with God through Jesus Christ. But there's more to having a comprehensive sense of peace in your life than just having peace with God. Many people have peace with God but still lack a sense of well-being because they have not made peace with who God has created them to be. Some people look down on themselves and never really rejoice in how God wired them up.

Underlying the entire fabric of their daily life is an "if only" mentality. If only I looked different. If only I had a more colorful personality. If only I had different abilities. If only I were in a different situation. People who think like this are wasting precious time and energy refusing to work with the raw materials God gave them. As a result, they are unhappy, insecure, and unfulfilled. God's P_2 peace can reconcile us to ourselves and bring a healthy acceptance about who we are. As a matter of fact, God's peace and presence can help us rejoice in who we are and to become thankful for where God has placed us in this life.

6

What are some of those "if only" areas in your life?

Ask someone to read Psalm 139:1–6 and 13–14. Pause to pray silently or as a group. Admit to God that you still live with some "if only" thoughts ruling your mind and heart. Begin thanking God for those very things you have always wished could be different.

Not focused on god.;

7

Take time as a group to communicate what you appreciate about how God has made each person. Have group members volunteer to communicate something they value about other group members. Be sure to focus on those things that are part of how God has made them.

Phyllis

Read Snapshot "Peace with Others"

PEACE WITH OTHERS

You can be reconciled with God and to yourself, but if you're waging war with a brother or a sister, your peace can still be forfeited. In other words, God wants you to be at P_2 peace with every person in your life. Even nonbelievers can learn how to be civil with one another and experience P_1 peace, but when you receive Christ, the Holy Spirit is going to do something supernatural in your life twenty-four hours a day, seven days a week. He's going to nudge, urge, inspire, and give you the courage not only to stop fighting with certain people, but He's also going to work you over until finally you make that phone call, write that letter, set up that appointment, and say those simple words, "Let's be brothers again" or "Let's be sisters again."   *S. School lesson....*

It's not enough to just lay the weapons down, go our own way, and avoid each other at gatherings. That's peace as the world knows it. The Holy Spirit moves you to a whole new level of peace—a peace that involves reconciliation.

8

With whom are you presently not at peace?

What is it going to take to have P_1 peace with that person?

What is it going to take to have P$_2$ peace with that person?

How can you work together as a group to support each other in your peace-making efforts?

PUTTING YOURSELF IN THE PICTURE

FEARFULLY AND WONDERFULLY MADE

Take time in the coming week to memorize and reflect on Psalm 139:14:

> I praise you because I am fearfully and wonderfully made; your works are wonderful, I know that full well.

BUILDING BRIDGES OF PEACE WITH OTHERS

Identify one or two people with whom you need to establish P$_2$ peace. Commit to do the following things:

1. Pray for that person daily. Pray for God's goodness to fill his or her life.
2. Pray for yourself daily as you seek to restore peace to this relationship. Pray for your attitude and actions to be filled with the love and peace of God.
3. Set a specific time to communicate with this person. During this time, be ready to let them know that you desire to have P$_1$ peace with them—an absence of conflict and fighting—and that you also want to have P$_2$ peace—a healthy, loving, God-filled friendship.
4. Even if the person chooses not to reconcile at this time, continue to pray for that person and for God to do His work in both of you. Pray that God would help you accept the things you cannot control and keep you open for ways in which you can make a difference.
5. Have another follower of Christ pray for you and keep you accountable to follow through on this commitment.

PATIENCE

REFLECTIONS FROM SESSION 3

1. For those who memorized and reflected on Psalm 139:14, how has this reminder from God helped you grow in your ability to be at peace with yourself?
2. If you have been working at building a bridge of peace ✓ G.D with someone, describe how this has changed your heart and impacted this relationship.

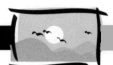

THE BIG PICTURE

I love watching Sunday afternoon football games on TV. Some time back, it was halftime of a Chicago Bears football game, and the Bears had a slim lead. I thought, as long as I had a few minutes, I would dash to the convenience store and pick up a paper before the second half started. I took off out of the door and drove very quickly to the store. I left the car running out front, grabbed the paper off the rack, and took the next place in line. I quickly noticed there were four people in front of me and only one person working at the counter. I would have skirted around them and put a dollar on the counter, but I only had a five.

While I stood in line, I impatiently tapped my foot and began watching every move the cashier made. I thought, *She could work a lot faster if she were standing up instead of sitting on a stool.* Then she began to chat with one of the customers in front of me. I thought, *Oh great, a social butterfly. I'm going to be here all day.* Then I started eyeing each person in front of me to see what they had in their hands. I was trying to determine if they had any trouble items. Everybody in line seemed fine except the guy immediately in front of me, who was holding a bag of chips.

I always become suspicious if someone stands in front of me with only a bag of chips because it looks too much like *part* of a lunch. As I stood there impatiently, my worst fear came true. He did something that is perfectly legal, but very irritating. He ordered a ham and cheese sandwich to be made in the deli next to the cashier station. With only one cashier working, that meant anybody waiting in line behind that guy (including me) might as well crawl into a corner and take a nap because this was going to take awhile. "What kind of bread, white or wheat? What kind of ham would you like? Baked ham, smoked ham, country ham? Would you like thick sliced or thin sliced? What kind of cheese would you like?" As the questions continued to go back and forth, I was churning inside. It felt like everyone was moving in slow motion!

When the man finally got his sandwich and left, I paid for my paper, glared at the cashier, drove home, slammed the door, and sat down frustrated because I had missed the start of the second half of the game. As I reflect back on that five-minute delay, I realize that it destroyed my entire emotional equilibrium. One person ordering one sandwich and my day had been ruined.

A WIDE ANGLE VIEW

1   What is one of your pet peeves that pushes your impatience button?

A BIBLICAL PORTRAIT

Read Psalm 103:8–12

2   What do you learn about the character of God in this psalm? *Infinite ; All forgiving; all loving. He does not harbor his anger forever;*

How do you feel when you read these words? Small. Why can't I be so kind & forgiving to others.

3

How do you see the patience of God in this passage?

When was a time you have experienced this kind of divine
patience in your life? When Aidan was so sick & I had to sit & be ċ him/ or when I wanted to do something & have & all I was called to do was Be ċ Aidan. He taught me that patience!

SHARPENING THE FOCUS

Read Snapshot "When Patience Runs Out, Watch Out!"

WHEN PATIENCE RUNS OUT, WATCH OUT!

When patience runs out and a husband launches a verbal attack on his wife, he wounds her. Later he hopes that she'll forget those words, but she can't because they've been registered in her memory bank and burned on her heart. The same thing happens when a wife gives her husband a "you're pathetic" look that cuts deeper than words. Or when an exasperated father says to his little boy, "Look, just hit the ball, will you? All the other kids your age can hit the ball. What's wrong with you?" Or when a mother says to her daughter, "Just get out of the kitchen. All you're capable of doing is making a mess." Or when an employer says to an employee, "Why do I even pay you? I can do better than that. Get out of my way."

When patience wears thin, the pastor says to the congregation, "Nobody around here is committed like I am." And the congregation says to its pastor, "Where did you learn to preach, anyway?" When patience runs out, watch out! Someone is going to get hurt.

4

Break into groups of two or three and answer these questions:

- Tell a story of how you were hurt by someone's impatience.

- How could patience in that situation have spared you from pain and hurt?

- Describe a time you hurt someone else because of your impatience.

- How could you have behaved differently and spared someone else from needless hurt?

Still in your small group of two or three, take a moment to pray for each other. Pray for healing in the lives of those who have experienced pain or hurt at the hands of someone who was impatient with them. Next, allow a time for confession and forgiveness of the times you have hurt others through your impatience.

Read Snapshot "God's Patience with Unbelievers"

GOD'S PATIENCE WITH UNBELIEVERS

As you grow in your knowledge of God and the Bible, you will be struck with the depth of God's patience toward rebellious, sinful, pride-filled people. The beginning chapters of Genesis all the way through the book of Revelation contain record after record of human rebellion and running from God. As a righteous and holy God, He could have eliminated all offenders—exterminated the entire race. However, God still loves His children and seeks to enter into a love relationship with them.

In Psalm 103:8 we read these words, "The LORD is compassionate and gracious, slow to anger, abounding in love." Other passages call Him a long-suffering God. When we remember His patience with us and with all who are still running from Him, we are called to share in the same loving patience God shows.

5

How did God show you His patience before you were a follower of Christ?

How could this fact impact the way you respond to nonbelievers who annoy you with their decidedly "unspiritual" lifestyles?

Read Snapshot "God's Patience with Believers"

GOD'S PATIENCE WITH BELIEVERS

God was not only patient with you before you were a follower of Christ, but He has been patient with you every day since you became a Christian. When I think of God's patience with believers, I think of the apostle Peter. I'm always amazed at how Peter tried the patience of Jesus, and how Jesus just kept on loving him. One minute Peter would say, "You are the Christ. The Son of the living God. I'll die for you," and then next minute, he would say, "Jesus who? I don't know the man!" One minute he would be walking on water, and the next he would be drowning in doubt and fear. In the midst of all of this, Jesus put up with Peter—the picture of inconsistency.

God grows patience in our lives as we see His great patience with us. When we picture how long-suffering and patient God has been with us it seems to just melt away our impatience. God slowly softens our hard hearts and quietly replaces them with an attitude of tolerance, understanding, and forbearance.

---

6 In what area of your character has God shown His patience to you *since* you have been a follower of Christ?

How does focusing on God's patience help you grow in patience with others?

7 What is one situation in your life in which you are struggling with impatience?

How can your group members pray for you and support you as you seek to yield to the supernatural power of the Holy Spirit by being patient in this situation?

PUTTING YOURSELF IN THE PICTURE

PATIENCE ON PAPER

Take time to remember the depth of God's patience with you. Reflect on very specific times God has had to extend His great patience to you. Write down not only what you did that needed God's patience, but also how He showed mercy and patience when you did not deserve it.

God's patience *before* I was a follower of Christ:

- _____

- _____

- _____

- _____

- _____

God's patience *since* I have been a follower of Christ:

- _____

- _____

- _____

- _____

- _____

List the things you are often impatient about:

- _____

- _____

- _____

- _____

- _____

Take time to compare the kinds of things God has overlooked in your life to the things that so irritate you and cause you to be impatient. Pray for a softened and changed heart, and for the Spirit of God to grow the fruit of patience in your life.

SENSITIVITY

REFLECTIONS FROM SESSION 4

1. If you took time since the last meeting to remember the depth of God's patience in your life, how has this reflection impacted your commitment to be patient with others?

THE BIG PICTURE

Little Johnny can't believe it. The first five years of his life have been filled with love, affirmation, birthday parties, Christmas presents, puppies, and cartoons. Now it's the third day of kindergarten and Bobby, the class bully, calls him a "fathead." After supper Johnny timidly asks his dad, "What's a fathead?" After Johnny relates the whole story, his dad gives a stirring speech about life in the big city and the harsh realities of kindergarten. He finishes his speech by saying, "Life is tough, Johnny, and it's only going to get tougher. You're going to have to toughen up if you're going to survive."

Three years later, Johnny comes home after a neighborhood football game with a bloody nose. He says to his dad, "Jim got mad and slugged me just because our team won. I thought Jim was my friend." Dad, once again, rises to the occasion and tells little Johnny that all young guys get punched in the nose. It's a part of growing up. He repeats the proverb: "Johnny, I told you once, I'll tell you again. Life is tough. It's only going to get tougher, and you're going to have to toughen up if you're going to survive."

In high school Johnny watches the upperclassmen punch each other for fun, slamming each other into lockers and then pretending it doesn't hurt. He watches them spit, smoke, curse, and drink. He listens as they call unattractive girls "dogs" and the weaker guys "nerds" and "wimps" and other colorful names. Johnny finally understands what his dad was referring to earlier. Life is tough, and it seems to get a whole lot tougher over time. Johnny reasons to himself, "I better toughen up if I'm going to survive this life."

When Johnny enters the marketplace it doesn't take long for him to discover why veterans of that system call it a jungle. To Johnny's utter amazement he learns that lying is standard operating procedure. Exaggeration is the only way to advertise and promote. Deception is the best way to gain information. Backstabbing is a form of professional recreation. Loyalty isn't found in the marketplace dictionary. And profit isn't everything—it's the *only* thing. Relationships are kept at a surface level. Job security is as real as your last paycheck.

Johnny shivers and reasons quietly, "Life is tough, and it seems to be getting more so. Only the tough seem to survive." He looks suspiciously at all the people in his life and asks, "What's his angle? What's her game? What's in it for them? How can I cover myself?" Without even noticing it, Johnny has built a fortress of protection around his heart and life. Life may be tough, but he is tougher. Nothing can hurt him.

A WIDE ANGLE VIEW

1 In this story, little Johnny was told, "Life is tough, and it's only gonna get tougher. So you better toughen up if you are going to survive." What are some similar messages you heard as you were growing up?

A BIBLICAL PORTRAIT

Read 2 Samuel 10:1–5

2 How does David show a tender and sensitive heart in this story:

- Toward the king of the Ammonites?

- Toward his own men who were humiliated?

Read Snapshot "A Tender-hearted King"

A TENDER-HEARTED KING

How can the Holy Spirit make a tough person tender? In the Old Testament we meet a man who was tough and tender at the same time. The Bible called him courageous, a mighty man of valor, one of the greatest warriors of all time, a great military strategist, a risk taker. His name was King David, and he was no stranger to the school of hard knocks. He had grown up as the youngest of many brothers. He had been on King Saul's hit list for many years. Many foreign kings wanted him killed. Later in his life, his own son attempted to have him killed and started a civil war to take David's throne. David knew how tough life could be. However, David maintained a tender and sensitive heart in the midst of a tough world.

3 In David's day and in our day, some people would say, "Tender-heartedness and sensitivity is a sign of weakness!" How do you respond to this statement?

How was Jesus an example of tender-heartedness when He lived on earth?

SHARPENING THE FOCUS

Read Snapshot "Empathizing Easily"

EMPATHIZING EASILY

The Holy Spirit's goal is to make every single follower of Christ a sensitive person. His first step is to help us learn how to empathize easily. You see, insensitive people have a reflex reaction when they see others who are hurting. They say, "It's not my problem. Glad it didn't happen to me. I hope he lands on his feet. I hope she pulls through it. Time has a way of healing things." Insensitive people don't empathize. They don't walk in someone else's shoes. They are unaffected by the plight of other people.

But the Holy Spirit won't settle for that if you're a Christian. The Holy Spirit is going to work you over on the inside and remind you that God was deeply moved by your plight. God felt so deeply that He sent His only Son to die for you. The Holy Spirit is also going to remind you that God is still moved by your prayers and your cries for help. Over time, God's Spirit will soften your heart, slow you down, increase your vulnerability, and teach you to empathize with others in the middle of their pain. He'll urge you to walk in someone else's shoes so you can feel what it is that other people are experiencing and facing.

4

What situations has God placed you in that have softened your heart to the hurts and needs of others?

Read Snapshot "Participating Personally"

PARTICIPATING PERSONALLY

David knew there was really no substitute for personal participation in someone else's pain. He could have ignored the news of how his messengers had been publicly humiliated. After all, he was a busy man. He had a kingdom to run. But David knew some situations demand personal involvement, so he reached out to these men and cared for them. Not only did his heart soften toward them, but he entered into their pain and felt the shame they were feeling.

So often we would prefer to do our mercy work by mail. We would rather send a card or a check or a word of encouragement. And those can be appropriate means of expressing concern. But after awhile, the Holy Spirit will make you start to empathize, and then you'll want to actually participate personally in the pain of another human being.

5

Describe a time someone reached out to you and participated in your pain or time of struggle. How did you feel?

How did you experience the love of God through this person?

6

Tell about a time God moved your heart so much that you *had to* actively participate in someone else's pain.

What happened in your heart that moved you into action?

Read Snapshot "Assistance in Acting Appropriately"

ASSISTANCE IN ACTING APPROPRIATELY

When David heard of the public humiliation his friends experienced, he could have responded in a variety of ways. But David said to the men, "I know you have been greatly humiliated. Therefore, go to Jericho until your beards grow back. Take the time you need so that you will suffer no additional humiliation." You see, the Holy Spirit not only helped David empathize and desire to participate in the pain of these men, but the Spirit also gave David assistance in knowing the appropriate course of action to take in this situation.

The Holy Spirit will also give you assistance in acting appropriately in difficult situations. We can be so worried about dropping our defenses and lowering our guard that we fail to do so. We fear what might happen if we empathize with others and get involved in their problems. But as you trust God, the Holy Spirit will give you exactly what you need to carry out the assignment He gives you. You will find yourself comforting people with words that are not your own. Listening with attentiveness that isn't typical. Confronting people with courage you never knew you had. Counseling people with wisdom that comes from the Spirit of God. Upholding people with strength beyond your own. You'll find yourself serving people with a tenderness that only comes through the supernatural power of the Holy Spirit.

7

Try to remember a time the Holy Spirit gave you just the right words or insight to help another person through a difficult situation.

How did you know these words and insight came from God and not from yourself?

8 In what situation do you sense the Holy Spirit prompting you to help someone, but you find yourself resisting?

What is it going to take for you to soften your heart and respond to the leading of the Spirit?

What can your group members do to encourage and support you in following the Spirit's leading in this area of your life?

PUTTING YOURSELF IN THE PICTURE

OUR GREATEST EXAMPLE OF SENSITIVITY

When Jesus walked on the face of this earth He showed a depth of sensitivity and tenderness that is an example to each one of us. He was, at the same time, strong and uncompromising. Jesus is the perfect example of strength and sensitivity. Take time to read part of the Gospel of Luke and write down as many examples of Jesus' tenderness as you can find.

Passage	Jesus' Example of Tenderness
_____	_____
_____	_____
_____	_____
_____	_____
_____	_____
_____	_____
_____	_____

Pray for the Holy Spirit to give you the tender heart of Jesus. Pray also for courage to move into action and participate in the pain of others when the Holy Spirit moves your heart.

A COMMITMENT TO ACTION

Picture someone or some situation where God is seeking to soften your heart and make you more sensitive:

God wants me to grow more sensitive towards

_____ .

Walk through three steps of seeking to grow in sensitivity:

1. Pray for the Holy Spirit to help you learn to empathize with those who are hurting in this situation. Seek to place yourself in their situation and ask God to soften your heart toward their pain and hurt.
2. Make yourself available to participate in the pain of this person. Identify a specific time in your schedule when you will reach out and care for this person.
3. Pray for the Holy Spirit to give you insight and wisdom to know exactly how you should enter into this situation.

What specific action do you feel the Holy Spirit is prompting you to take?

FAITHFULNESS

REFLECTIONS FROM SESSION 5

1. If you took time to study part of the Gospel of Luke and wrote down your insights, discuss one or two things you learned about the sensitivity of Jesus to the hurts and needs of others. How has your learning impacted your desire to have a tender and sensitive heart like Jesus?

2. If you made a commitment to express tenderness toward another person, tell your group how you did in keeping this commitment. How did the person you cared for respond to your tenderness and sensitivity?

THE BIG PICTURE

Over the years I have asked various groups of people to write down their answer to this question: *What trait in other people do you dislike the most?* Or, I'll phrase it another way: *What flaw in other people's characters do you find most difficult to tolerate?* Guess what always seems to appear near the top of the list? Unfaithfulness!

People describe unfaithfulness differently. Some say, "I hate it when people say one thing and do another." Or, "It drives me crazy when people promise to come through and they fall through." Or, "I can't stand it when people say 'count me in,' but then when the chips are down they say, 'count me out.'" Whatever the definition, these folks are describing unfaithfulness. They're describing a person who is undependable, disloyal, inconsistent, or not true to his or her word.

I think we would all agree that unfaithfulness is not only distasteful, but it is a disease running rampant in our culture. "Faithfulness" almost sounds like a foreign word to many people today. Thousands of years ago Solomon said, "A faithful man who can find?" (Prov. 20:6) I guess some things don't change over time. It is still hard to find a man or woman who is faithful.

These days, it seems faithfulness has lost its importance. We would all probably have to strain our memories to think of people who have worked faithfully at the same company for twenty-five years. It's getting tougher and tougher to hold up examples of couples who have been happily married for thirty or forty years. And the days when a professional athlete was committed to a team or club for a lifetime are long gone. We don't often hear about friendship that spans a lifetime. Let's face it, faithfulness has fallen on hard times.

A WIDE ANGLE VIEW

1 Describe in detail *one* of the following people who has modeled faithfulness to you:
- A family member
- A teacher
- A pastor or church leader
- A friend

What were some of the characteristics that marked this person's life?

A BIBLICAL PORTRAIT

Read Proverbs 20:6–7; Revelation 2:8–11

Read Snapshot "What Is Faithfulness?"

WHAT IS FAITHFULNESS?

Faithfulness means you stick to a commitment after the shine wears off. Faithfulness means you keep your word even though complications arise and promise-keeping costs you more than you thought it would. Faithfulness means you keep saying no, a thousand times if you must, to the temptation of cutting a corner and taking the easy way out. Faithfulness means you keep working through relational problems rather than disposing of the relationship like yesterday's trash. Faithfulness means you see a project through to the bitter end. Faithfulness means you refuse to jump ship even when the waves of adversity are splashing over the decks of your marriage, your relationship with your children, your vocation, your ministry, or your relationship with others. Faithfulness means you stay true to your relationship with Jesus Christ no matter what it costs you.

2

Both of these passages call followers of Christ to be
faithful. Take a moment for personal reflection and
then write down four things that you believe are signs
of a faithful follower of Christ.

A faithful follower of Christ:

- _____

- _____

- _____

- _____

*Read one or more items from your list to the group and
explain why you feel these are critical elements of what it
means to be faithful as a follower of Christ.*

3

In Revelation 2:10 we are called to be faithful "even to
the point of death." How do you react when you read
these words?

*How can we live out this level of faithfulness even when our
lives are not in physical danger?*

SHARPENING THE FOCUS

Read Snapshot "Great Is Thy Faithfulness"

GREAT IS THY FAITHFULNESS

The first step in the process of God transforming you into a more faithful person is that the Holy Spirit will convince you of God's unfailing, unquestionable faithfulness toward you.

As a kid growing up in the church, we used to sing "Great Is Thy Faithfulness, " a song that celebrates the depths of God's mercy and His unwavering faithfulness to His children. As a young boy, I would look around and watch others as they sang this hymn. Most of the kids would be looking out into space, winking at their friends, and getting into trouble. The adolescents and college-age students would sort of mouth the words mechanically. The young married couples and the middle-aged people would be singing that song with some meaning and heart. But the older people in that church were singing from the depths of their heart. I can still recall watching some of them singing at the top of their lungs, "All I had needed Thy hand has provided," and at the end, the song building to a crescendo, "Great is Thy faithfulness, Lord unto me!" They sang that song with a conviction that marked my life.

---

4 If you were to sing "Great Is Thy Faithfulness," what would you be thinking about? How has God shown His faithfulness to you at *one* of these times:

- Before you knew who Jesus was
- This week
- This year
- Over your life as a follower of Christ

5 What hymn or worship song helps you remember God's faithfulness, and what is it about this song that helps you focus on God's faithfulness in your life?

Read Snapshot "As Good As Our Word"

AS GOOD AS OUR WORD

We have all witnessed a wedding. The bride and groom stand at the altar before God, a pastor, family, and friends and make a public vow to be faithful to their spouse. They give their word before heaven and earth! This is serious business. But God expects us to be faithful even in the little things. We don't have to stand in a church and make a formal vow before God and witnesses for God to expect us to keep our word. When we say, "I'll do it," we better do it. When we say, "I'll be there," we better show up. When we give our word, people should have no question about what we mean. As followers of Christ we should be as good as our word. This kind of faithfulness should not be seen as exceptional behavior of super-saints. It is simply the way God calls us to live out our faith . . . faithfully!

6 How can a lack of faithfulness have a negative impact in *one* of these areas:

- Your friendships
- Your family
- Your faith
- Your vocation

How can a deep commitment to faithfulness have a positive impact in one of these same areas?

7 In what relationship or situation do you need to commit yourself to live with a deeper level of faithfulness?

What practical things need to happen for you to develop faithfulness in this situation or relationship?

How can your small group members encourage you, pray for you, and spur you on in this area of your life?

PUTTING YOURSELF IN THE PICTURE

Faithful No Matter What!

Take time in the coming week to memorize and reflect on Revelation 2:10:

> Be faithful, even to the point of death, and I will give you the crown of life.

Thanks to the Faithful

Take time in the coming week to contact someone who has been a consistent example of faithfulness. Call them, write them a note, or take them out for lunch. Use this opportunity to thank them for their faithfulness and let them know how God has used them to mark your life and challenge you to be more faithful.

LEADER'S NOTES

Leading a Bible discussion—especially for the first time—can make you feel both nervous and excited. If you are nervous, realize that you are in good company. Many biblical leaders, such as Moses, Joshua, and the apostle Paul, felt nervous and inadequate to lead others (see, for example, 1 Cor. 2:3). Yet God's grace was sufficient for them, just as it will be for you.

Some excitement is also natural. Your leadership is a gift to the others in the group. Keep in mind, however, that other group members also share responsibility for the group. Your role is simply to stimulate discussion by asking questions and encouraging people to respond. The suggestions listed below can help you to be an effective leader.

PREPARING TO LEAD

1. Ask God to help you understand and apply the passage to your own life. Unless that happens, you will not be prepared to lead others.
2. Carefully work through each question in the study guide. Meditate and reflect on the passage as you formulate your answers.
3. Familiarize yourself with th Leader's Notes for each session. These will help you understand the purpose of the session and will provide valuable information about the questions in the session. The Leader's Notes are not intended to be read to the group. These notes are primarily for your use as a group leader and for your preparation. However, when you find a section that relates well to your group, you may want to read a brief portion or encourage them to read this section at another time.
4. Pray for the various members of the group. Ask God to use these sessions to make you better disciples of Jesus Christ.
5. Before the first session, make sure each person has a study guide. Encourage them to prepare beforehand for each session.

LEADING THE SESSION

1. Begin the session on time. If people realize that the session begins on schedule, they will work harder to arrive on time.

2. At the beginning of your first time together, explain that these sessions are designed to be discussions, not lectures. Encourage everyone to participate, but realize some may be hesitant to speak during the first few sessions.

3. Don't be afraid of silence. People in the group may need time to think before responding.

4. Avoid answering your own questions. If necessary, rephrase a question until it is clearly understood. Even an eager group will quickly become passive and silent if they think the leader will do most of the talking.

5. Encourage more than one answer to each question. Ask, "What do the rest of you think?" or "Anyone else?" until several people have had a chance to respond.

6. Try to be affirming whenever possible. Let people know you appreciate their insights into the passage.

7. Never reject an answer. If it is clearly wrong, ask, "Which verse led you to that conclusion?" Or let the group handle the problem by asking them what they think about the question.

8. Avoid going off on tangents. If people wander off course, gently bring them back to the passage being considered.

9. Conclude your time together with conversational prayer. Ask God to help you apply those things that you learned in the session.

10. End on time. This will be easier if you control the pace of the discussion by not spending too much time on some questions or too little on others.

We encourage all small group leaders to use *Leading Life-Changing Small Groups* (Zondervan) by Bill Donahue and the Willow Creek Small Group Team while leading their group. Developed and used by Willow Creek Community Church, this guide is an excellent resource for training and equipping followers of Christ to effectively lead small groups. It includes valuable information on how to utilize fun and creative relationship-building exercises for your group; how to plan your meeting; how to share the leadership load by identifying, developing, and working with an "apprentice leader"; and how to find creative ways to do group prayer. In addition, the book includes material and tips on handling potential conflicts and difficult personalities, forming group covenants, inviting new members, improving listening skills, studying the Bible, and much more. Using *Leading Life-Changing Small Groups* will help you create a group that members love to be a part of.

Now let's discuss the different elements of this small group study guide and how to use them for the session portion of your group meeting.

The Big Picture

Each session will begin with a short story or overview of the lesson theme. This is called "The Big Picture" because it introduces the central theme of the session. You will need to read this section as a group or have group members read it on their own before discussion begins. Here are three ways you can approach this section of the small group session:

- As the group leader, read this section out loud for the whole group and then move into the questions in the next section, "A Wide Angle View." (You might read the first week, but then use the other two options below to encourage group involvement.)
- Ask a group member to volunteer to read this section for the group. This allows another group member to participate. It is best to ask someone in advance to give them time to read over the section before reading it to the group. It is also good to ask someone to volunteer, and not to assign this task. Some people do not feel comfortable reading in front of a group. After a group member has read this section out loud, move into the discussion questions.
- Allow time at the beginning of the session for each person to read this section silently. If you do this, be sure to allow enough time for everyone to finish reading so they can think about what they've read and be ready for meaningful discussion.

A Wide Angle View

This section includes one or more questions that move the group into a general discussion of the session topic. These questions are designed to help group members begin discussing the topic in an open and honest manner. Once the topic of the lesson has been established, move on to the Bible passage for the session.

A Biblical Portrait

This portion of the session includes a Scripture reading and one or more questions that help group members see how the theme of the session is rooted and based in biblical teaching. The Scripture reading can be handled just like "The Big Picture" section: You can read it for the group, have a group member read it, or allow time for silent reading. Make sure everyone has a Bible or that you have Bibles available for those who need them. Once you have read the passage, ask the question(s) in this section so that group members can dig into the truth of the Bible.

SHARPENING THE FOCUS

The majority of the discussion questions for the session are in this section. These questions are practical and help group members apply biblical teaching to their daily lives.

SNAPSHOTS

The "Snapshots" in each session help prepare group members for discussion. These anecdotes give additional insight to the topic being discussed. Each "Snapshot" should be read at a designated point in the session. This is clearly marked in the session as well as in the Leader's Notes. Again, follow the same format as you do with "The Big Picture" section and the "Biblical Portrait" section: Either you read the anecdote, have a group member volunteer to read, or provide time for silent reading. However you approach this section, you will find these anecdotes very helpful in triggering lively dialogue and moving discussion in a meaningful direction.

PUTTING YOURSELF IN THE PICTURE

Here's where you roll up your sleeves and put the truth into action. This portion is very practical and action-oriented. At the end of each session there will be suggestions for one or two ways group members can put what they've just learned into practice. Review the action goals at the end of each session and challenge group members to work on one or more of them in the coming week.

You will find follow-up questions for the "Putting Yourself in the Picture" section at the beginning of the next week's session. Starting with the second week, there will be time set aside at the beginning of the session to look back and talk about how you have tried to apply God's Word in your life since your last time together.

PRAYER

You will want to open and close your small group with a time of prayer. Occasionally, there will be specific direction within a session for how you can do this. Most of the time, however, you will need to decide the best place to stop and pray. You may want to pray or have a group member volunteer to begin the lesson with a prayer. Or you might want to read "The Big Picture" and discuss the "Wide Angle View" questions before opening in prayer. In some cases, it might be best to open in prayer after you have read the Bible passage. You need to decide where you feel an opening prayer best fits for your group.

When opening in prayer, think in terms of the session theme and pray for group members (including yourself) to be responsive to the truth of Scripture and the working of the Holy Spirit. If you have seekers in your group (people investigating Christianity but not yet believers), be sensitive to your expectations for group prayer. Seekers may not yet be ready to take part in group prayer.

Be sure to close your group with a time of prayer as well. One option is for you to pray for the entire group. Or you might allow time for group members to offer audible prayers that others can agree with in their hearts. Another approach would be to allow a time of silence for one-on-one prayers with God and then to close this time with a simple "Amen."

LOVE

PHILIPPIANS 2:1—11

INTRODUCTION

There is a crisis in Christendom with regard to character. There are so many people who call themselves Christians and attend churches, but who don't have the kind of character that puts them squarely in the camp of those who know God in a personal way. People claim to know Christ and yet they live in ways contrary to the will and heart of Christ.

As Christ followers, we enter into a new life, a supernatural life empowered and led by the Spirit. When this happens, we can love others and put their needs and interests before our own because we have hearts that are filled with the love of God. This first session on the fruit of the Spirit will challenge you to look at how your life is being transformed by the power of the Holy Spirit.

THE BIG PICTURE

Take time to read this introduction with the group. There are suggestions for how this can be done in the beginning of the leader's section.

A WIDE ANGLE VIEW

Question One There are no right or wrong answers to this first question. The key is to allow group members to begin articulating their understanding of love. The meaning of love changes as we grow, and it is helpful to look back and see how our understanding of love has evolved throughout the years.

A BIBLICAL PORTRAIT

Read Philippians 2:1–11

Questions Two & Three This passage not only calls us to be loving in a sacrificial and selfless way, but it holds up the perfect example of Jesus Christ. As your group studies this passage, notice how Jesus did not only make us His top priority when He gave His life on the cross. He put us at the top of the list as He set aside the glory of heaven, emptied Himself, became a servant, took on human flesh, and died on the cross. His actions are our primary example as we seek to understand the meaning of love and model that love to a lost world.

SHARPENING THE FOCUS

Read Snapshot "Putting Others First, Even at One O'clock in the Morning" before Question 4

Question Four Every single day in our lives opportunities to show love come up in our homes, neighborhoods, offices, schools—everywhere we go. These opportunities are the moments of truth, when our interests, comforts, and pleasures are pitted against the interests of others. In such moments, we don't have to wait for a rush of sentimentality to overwhelm us. We just love. True love means we care for the interests of others above ourselves.

I remember an afternoon some years ago when I had finished a long workout at the "Y," and, after taking a shower, went into the steam room. As I entered, I saw three guys sitting on stools. My legs were rubbery and tired from running, so I claimed the one remaining empty stool and sat down. A few minutes later, the door opened and an elderly gentlemen walked in. He must have been in his late sixties or seventies. He looked for a stool to sit on, but there were none left.

He just stood there with his shoulders drooping. A few moments later, he began to lean against the wall of the steam room. My instinctual reaction was to think, *Boy, am I glad I got here first. Early bird gets the worm. You snooze you lose. Two more minutes and that could have been me with my rubbery legs standing against that wall.*

But while I was responding to my natural self-centeredness, God went into action and began to communicate to me: "Bill, here is an opportunity to put someone else's need before your own. Here is a golden opportunity to treat someone else as more important than yourself. Here is a chance to show real love."

While the Spirit was talking, I just shook my head and wondered, *Why didn't I think of that? I'm so focused on my own concerns, interests, and comfort, that my basic, natural instinct is self-centeredness.*

After the Spirit had done His part and alerted me to the opportunity, I sat on my stool and began to argue with myself. *But I don't want to take advantage of this opportunity*, I thought. *I like this stool. I got here first. My legs are tired.* But the Spirit kept working in my heart, urging me to take action. He said, "Come on, Bill. Do the right thing. Put someone else first. Show My love." Finally the Holy Spirit played His trump card. He said, "All right, Hybels. You serve a God who owed you nothing but gave you everything. The Father, in His grace, treated you as a very important person and put your needs in front of His. He sent His Son as a Savior for you. And that Savior took your punishment and shed His blood and opened His arms to you and forgave you and cleansed you and adopted you into the family and gave you brothers and sisters in the hope of eternal life. Now, don't you think you can give up a stool?" In this practical life situation, God let me know my role: Show love.

Read Snapshot "The Power of the Spirit" before Question 5

Questions Five & Six The first thing the Holy Spirit is going to do in our lives with regard to love is to alert us to unique opportunities to put someone else's interests and needs ahead of our own. You see, without the Holy Spirit piquing our interests, without Him capturing our attention in those everyday, mundane moments of life, we would miss those opportunities. Without the work of the Spirit, we would be hopelessly self-centered, constantly saying, "Me! My! Mine!" But the Holy Spirit is faithful. If we are open to His promptings and His presence, He will begin to whisper, "Here's an opportunity. Show My love by putting others before yourself."

Every time we are alerted to an opportunity, every time we are urged to take action, every time we are reminded of God's love toward us, we are given a chance to be knocked off our lofty perch of self-centeredness. A little more of our old self, our natural instinct, dies. You see, every time we cooperate with the work of the Holy Spirit as He attempts to transform us from self-centered people to others-centered people, God says, "That's the way that I want My children to act."

Not only will we sense God's approval, we will also sense an affirmation from the people we serve. If they ask us why we live the way we do, we can tell them, "I'm just hoping you can feel the love of God the way I feel it in my life." When they see something different, we can let them know that difference is a love that comes from a God who cares about us and who cares about them.

**Read Snapshot "God's Example of Love"
before Question 7**

Question Seven You might be thinking, *I try to live this way,
and I seem to fail more than I succeed.* Well, I have fantastic news
for you. Our God is totally committed to transforming self-
centered people into others-centered people. You see, God
wants nothing more than to produce His fruit and character in
your life. He desires to supernaturally transform your character throughout your Christian life. He wants to assist you in
winning battles you could never win on your own. He knows
that love arrests people and registers profoundly in people's
minds, and that it opens up doors of opportunity for conver-
sations about eternal matters.

Question Eight After allowing time for group members to
communicate where they most struggle in offering self-
sacrificing love, take time for group members to pray for
each other.

PUTTING YOURSELF IN THE PICTURE

Tell group members you will be providing time at the beginning of the next meeting for them to discuss how they have
put their faith into action. Let them tell their stories. However,
don't limit their interaction to the two options provided.
They may have put themselves into the picture in some other
way as a result of your study. Allow for honest and open
communication.

Also, be clear that there will not be any kind of a "test" or
forced reporting. All you are going to do is allow time for
people to volunteer to talk about how they have applied what
they learned in your last study. Some group members will feel
pressured if they think you are going to make everyone provide a "report." You don't want anyone to skip the next group
because they are afraid of having to say they did not follow
up on what they learned from the prior session. Focus instead
on providing a place for honest communication without cre-
ating pressure and fear of being embarrassed.

Every session from this point on will open with a look back at
the "Putting Yourself in the Picture" section of the previous
session.

JOY

JOHN 15:9—11

INTRODUCTION

All of us hunger for joy. There is not one person on the face of this earth who does not want to live a joy-filled life. Yet, so many people seem to live a joyless existence. In an effort to help those who are going through the "blues," many people line up to give words of advice. Some are merely "armchair experts" who give simple answers to complex questions. There are also the psychological experts who come with their insights. Though helpful, their answers don't completely solve our problems or fill our longings for joy. But when God speaks, He tells us where we can discover true joy.

This session helps us discover the source of our joy. When we enter into a transforming relationship with Christ, He places us in a community of loving people who share our desire to follow Him. Then He gives us a purpose in life and a reason for living. Along with this He gives us a hope for today and for eternity that no one can take away. When we have these things, we discover a joy that is so deep it goes beyond anything this world has to offer. This is the supernatural joy that comes only from the Holy Spirit.

THE BIG PICTURE

Take time to read this introduction with the group. There are suggestions for how this can be done in the beginning of the leader's section.

A WIDE ANGLE VIEW

Question One Allow time for open conversation about those things that bring joy and those things that take it away. Remember, each person will have a different joy quotient. Some will speak endlessly about what brings them joy and others will express grief over the many things that rob them of true joy. The key is to allow open and honest dialogue about joy.

A Biblical Portrait

Read John 15:9–11

Questions Two & Three Some group members will have clear and profound memories of how their life was joyless before knowing Christ. Others may have known the love of Christ from their childhood and may have a difficult time identifying a time of not knowing Him. Be sure to affirm those who came to faith early in life. Their journey of faith is just as rich as the person who had a dramatic conversion later in life. For those who have known the love of God from their childhood, invite them to communicate how their joy has grown deeper over the years.

God says in His Word that He wants joy to be a distinguishing mark of a Christian. He says in Galatians 5:22–25 that His Spirit is going to work twenty-four hours a day to produce joy in our lives. In John 15:11, Jesus says that He wants to make our joy full and complete. In Psalm 23, the psalmist says that God has made our cup to overflow. And in a sense, God is saying, "I want My children to explode with joy. I want it to run over. I want to give them so much joy that they must sing. They must dance. They must be creative. They must whistle and laugh and smile. I want their joy to snap the heads of people who live in a joyless society so that one by one, the question will be asked to My children, 'Where do you get your joy?'"

Sharpening the Focus

Read Snapshot "The Armchair Experts" before Question 4

Question Four Armchair experts are usually well-meaning and well-intentioned, but their suggestions tend to sound hollow and simplistic. They offer fast temporary relief from the symptoms of sorrow, but their advice is usually worth about what you paid for it: Nothing. Their advice usually focuses on that which is external and circumstantial. They would define joy as problem-free living, and most of us know that there's much more to joy than the absence of conflict. There are many people out there who don't have too many things going wrong in their lives, but who still don't have joy. We may occasionally get a valuable pearl of insight from an armchair expert, but most of the time their insight is simply not very helpful.

Read Snapshot "The Psychological Experts" before Question 5

Question Five William Glasser was the founder of reality therapy. He says, "From birth to old age, we need to love and be loved. Throughout our lives, our health and our happiness will depend on our ability to do so. To either love or allow ourselves to be loved is not enough. We must do both." He also says, "When we cannot satisfy our total need for love, we will, without fail, suffer and react with many familiar psychological symptoms from mild discomfort to anxiety to depression or complete withdrawal from the world around us."

What is Glasser saying? After studying people for a long time, he's saying that the most essential ingredient necessary to acquire a sense of joy and happiness is the presence of significant love relationships. Now, that rings true to me. Glasser is saying, in a sense, "If you're ever going to feel joy, you must feel love from other people." Some of the most continually sorrowful people I know are those who have grown up questioning the love commitment of their parents and other important people in their lives. And some of the most joyful people I know are those who have grown up in an environment of love and support. They seem to go at life with a head start because they grew up in an environment of unquestioned love.

Viktor Frankl is an existential psychologist. He says, "Striving to find meaning in one's life is the primary motivational force of man." Frankl says, "This meaning is unique and specific in that it must, and can, be fulfilled by that man alone. And only when a person finds meaning in his life, will he find the significance that will provide him with satisfaction in his life." What is Viktor Frankl saying? He's suggesting that there might be something more crucial to happiness than the mere presence of love relationships. Frankl is saying that if you really want to have joy, you have to find your purpose. That when you find out why you're here, what you uniquely offer to society, what you, in particular, are skilled at doing, and what gives you a sense of accomplishment, you will then, and only then, experience joy and satisfaction.

This also rings true to me. Some of the most joyful people I know are those who have a cause, a crusade, a sense of destiny, a sense that their lives really matter. These people seem to march to an inner drumbeat. They have the bounce of certainty in their step. I know people like that and so do you. Some of these people may have troubled backgrounds, and some of them have few, if any, significant love relationships, but they seem to be satisfied, and I sense it's because they live with purpose.

Bruno Bettelheim makes a little different point. Bettelheim is a psychologist who survived imprisonment in a Nazi concentration camp. After all he suffered and faced, he insists you can't have joy without hope. When you lose hope, you lose joy. He observed utter joylessness in the prisoners in his camp who believed the repeated statements of the Nazi guards that there was no hope for them. He said that when there was no hope, these people became "walking corpses." Bettelheim is saying that significant relationships are fine and purpose in life is great, but neither means much if you have no hope for tomorrow. What people really need, if they want joy and happiness, is hope for a brighter future.

Bettelheim's words ring true to me as well. I have never met a hopeless person who was a happy person. Most hopeless people are miserable. I've talked to people who say that they're in a dead-end job situation and they're not happy. I talk to people who say, "Man, my marriage is dead. It has no future. Going home is like going to prison. It'll never change." These are miserable people.

But watch the transformation in those people's lives when an injection of hope is administered. Even a man with a dead-end job who all of a sudden sees a light at the end of the tunnel will say, "But there are some exciting opportunities where I am employed." His whole perspective changes because of hope. And I've seen people in dead-end marriages see the beginning of change in their spouse. Their whole perspective changes. They say, "Well, maybe there is something to be gained by perseverance in this relationship."

The truth is that we need all three: love relationships, purpose in life, and hope. And it is only when we have the life God offers that it's possible.

Read Snapshot "A Biblical Perspective" before Question 6

Question Six I remember how it broke my dad's heart when I left our family produce company to go into vocational ministry. He had such high hopes for me in the business world. After I left the marketplace, I went over and worked in a Christian youth organization putting little metal pieces in boxes. I can remember my dad coming to see me. It was hard for him to walk into the back of that little shipping department and see me standing next to two elderly women, working for minimum wage, doing a job that seemed so meaningless. He took me out to lunch, and he said, "I'll get you out of this place. You can have your old office back. Come on back home." And I said, "You know what, Dad? I'm happy. I really am. I don't figure I'll do this the rest of my life, but this is what God has for me now. I find meaning and value in what I am doing, I really do! And I'm happy. I'm thrilled doing what I'm doing because God's hand is on my life." By the time he left, he said, "That's more important to me than whether or not you stay in our company. I love you, and I want you to be happy." He saw that I had a purpose and it brought me joy, that was enough for him.

Question Eight The psalmist says, "Surely goodness and love will follow me all the days of my life," and after that, "I will dwell in the house of the LORD forever." The Holy Spirit, over time, is going to say to you, "You have a bright tomorrow. You don't think there's any light at the end of the long, dark tunnel. But there is." Someday, you're going to sing, "Oh death, where is your victory? Oh grave, where is your sting?" You will have hope in life, and you'll have hope in death.

Do you know what all this adds up to? When you have a significant relationship with the Lord and with others, when you have a purpose in life, and when you have hope for a bright tomorrow, you experience joy. God loves you so much, He has made it a priority in His life to produce joy in your life. By the supernatural work of the Holy Spirit He's already carrying out a well-laid plan for you. What we have to do is cooperate with Him. Listen to Him. Believe Him when He says there's hope in this life and in the next. You can bank on it.

PUTTING YOURSELF IN THE PICTURE

Challenge group members to take time in the coming week to use part or all of this application section as an opportunity for continued growth.

PEACE

JOHN 14:25—27;
ROMANS 5:1—2

INTRODUCTION

God won't be happy until each of us experiences both P_1 and P_2 peace. P_1 peace is the end of conflict and war-like behavior. It is a cease-fire kind of peace. P_2 peace is much deeper. It is the peace that comes when we know the love of God. P_2 peace leads to a healed, reconciled, and loving relationship. It is this kind of peace God wants us to experience with Him, with ourselves, and with each other. God won't rest until we experience deep and loving relationships. He is in the business of building P_2 peace in our lives.

THE BIG PICTURE

Take time to read this introduction with the group. There are suggestions for how this can be done in the beginning of the leader's section.

A WIDE ANGLE VIEW

Question One All of us have a sense of what it means to be at peace. Allow group members to express how they understand peace in various areas of life. Most of these responses will focus on P_1 peace. This is fine. The goal here is to get the pulse of how your group members understand peace.

A BIBLICAL PORTRAIT

Read John 14:25–27; Romans 5:1–2

Questions Two & Three In John 14:27 Jesus says, "Peace I leave with you; my peace I give you. I do not give to you as the world gives." This is an often-quoted verse, but like so many familiar verses, I find that in my own spirit, familiarity breeds confusion. I like the verse because it talks about God giving me peace. What, after all, is more direly needed in a world filled with strife, conflict, and tension than a sense of peace? The point of confusion comes when we try to define what we mean by peace. Jesus Himself said that His peace was different than the peace the world offers. His peace is deeper and lasting.

Romans 5:1 teaches that we are justified by faith. In this passage, the apostle Paul is telling us about a miracle. Being justified by faith means that once we have confessed our sins to Jesus Christ and asked Him to be our Savior and Leader, God says we have peace with Him. True believers have ultimate peace with God through Jesus Christ.

When we have given our lives to the Lord, confessed our sins, and asked Christ to be our Savior, we are justified by faith and we cease fighting with God. The battle is over. But what happens next? Does God go back to heaven and tend to the saints and the angels? Do we stay here on earth and go back to business as usual? Is Romans talking about a peaceable parting of the ways? Of course not! God's peace is not just an end of conflict; it is the beginning of a whole new relationship.

Paul is saying that if you want to know what life is all about, you've got to know P_2 peace. It's a better, deeper peace. A peace that not only involves the end of hostilities with another party but the dissipation of that spirit of hostility and the beginning of a spirit of acceptance and love, a spirit which ultimately leads to the achievement of a healed and reconciled relationship.

The great news of Christianity is not just that God no longer has a charge against us. It is not just that the battle is over. The great news of Christianity is that God has buried our sins in the depths of the sea. He has now drawn near to us and announced His great affection. He has adopted us into His own family, placing His Spirit inside of us. When this occurs, we supernaturally find our spirits attracted to the God for whom we once had no time. We were enemies, but now we are friends.

SHARPENING THE FOCUS

Read Snapshot "Peace with God" before Question 4

Questions Four & Five I still get a kick when I hear people who have come to know Christ as adults say, "I can't believe I actually enjoy sitting down and talking to people about God. This has to be cosmic humor." Sometimes they say, "It's just not like me." And I say, "That's right. It's not like you. Something supernatural is going on."

What has happened in these people's lives? P_2 peace is being established by a work of the Holy Spirit. Instead of always fighting God, they have found themselves wanting to cooperate with Him. This is what happens when we find real peace with God through Jesus Christ. Instead of trying to shut Him out, we find ourselves thinking about Him and wanting to dialogue with Him. Instead of complaining about what God has or has not done for us lately, we find ourselves saying, "You are a good God, and You have been good to me. I want to live for You, to worship You, to praise Your name." When we discover that desire in our heart, there's something supernatural happening.

When this happens we live with a sense of what the Bible refers to as "shalom": well-being, rightness, completeness. We discover the truth of what the prophet Isaiah said—God is committed to providing us with a quality of life or a sense of well-being that produces peace like a river (Isa. 48:18).

I don't know about you, but I've sat by a few rivers over the years. Rivers do something to me. Watching the consistent flow and seeing the soothing nature of the rippling water quiets my spirit. When I think that God has taken upon Himself the responsibility of producing that same kind of peace in our lives, I can't deny that He must love us beyond our wildest dreams.

Read Snapshot "Peace with Ourselves" before Question 6

Questions Six & Seven Someday the Holy Spirit, through constant persuasion and urging, is going to lead you to a point where you realize that you're a snowflake, not a flake. You're a snowflake in the sense that it has pleased God to make every person unique and wonderfully different—custom designed to fit His divine mosaic.

You will be much closer to characterizing the quality of your life as having peace like a river when you stop arguing with God about how He made you. Instead, start agreeing with the Holy Spirit and come to that place in your life where you actually, honestly say, "I'm unique. I'm wonderfully different from every other person in how I look, in my personality, and in how I function. I'm fearfully and wonderfully made. I'm custom designed by the hand of God."

It is easy to say, "I would enjoy life if I were made different physically. If I were taller or shorter, thinner or fatter, had more hair or less hair, a lighter or darker complexion." Or, "If only I had a different emotional makeup. I would like to be an easygoing, life-of-the-party type person, and I find myself being melancholy and introspective." Most of us wonder what life might be like if we had different abilities, more charisma, or greater athletic, speaking, or management skills. When we discover God's P_2 peace, we can finally rejoice in who God has made us and really live at peace with who we are.

These two discussion starters will help you discover and communicate openly about how God has made you. Pray for this time in your small group. It is hard to be honest about aspects of our appearance, personality, and life we wish we could change. Listen carefully to each other. Be honest about each person's struggles. Pray for each other. Give a word of encouragement to your group members.

Read Snapshot "Peace with Others" before Question 8

Question Eight Most of the people in your group, if not all of them, have a family member, someone at work, someone in their neighborhood, or someone in the church with whom they just can't get along. They wish they could, but they can't. The Holy Spirit is going to be working them over until they contact that person and say, "I don't just want to stop fighting. I don't want to just be civil. I want to be reconciled to you. I want a healed and loving relationship with you." The Spirit won't settle for anything less.

The final question in this session gives some group members a chance to tell their stories about how God has healed relationships in the past. These words will give hope for those who eagerly desire reconciliation in a broken relationship. Engage in a practical discussion about specific people with whom your group members seek to restore broken relationships.

Putting Yourself in the Picture

Challenge group members to take time in the coming week to use part or all of this application section as an opportunity for continued growth.

PATIENCE

PSALM 103:8—12

INTRODUCTION

Do you want to develop some strong relationships? It's going to require patience. Do you want to develop a great marriage? It's going to require patience. Do you want to succeed in the marketplace? You must have patience. Do you want to become all God would have you be as a follower of Christ? You will have to have the supernatural patience that only the Holy Spirit can provide.

God loves us so much that He can't stand to see the damage done to ourselves and others because of the loss of patience. He assumes responsibility out of His great love and says, "What you cannot do naturally, I will help you do supernaturally." The Holy Spirit is commissioned by God to work overtime for you with the goal of growing patience in your heart and life.

THE BIG PICTURE

Take time to read this introduction with the group. There are suggestions for how this can be done in the beginning of the leader's section.

A WIDE ANGLE VIEW

Question One Each of us can list many of the day-to-day frustrations of life that leave us uptight and impatient. Impatience crosses all demographic lines: rich and poor, white collar and blue collar, educated and uneducated, Christian and non-Christian, Democrat and Republican. Everyone is acquainted with impatience.

Allow group members to tell their stories and express their pet peeves. The more honest you begin this lesson, the deeper you will be able to go. Encourage honest expression of those things which push your own buttons and make you impatient.

What makes someone impatient varies from person to person. I've heard people say, "It's when I'm in a hurry and I have to get some cash, so I go to the drive-up window at the bank.

There's only one lane open, and the guy in front of me negotiates a second mortgage on his home from the front seat of his car. The canister goes back and forth so many times, it's hot to the touch when you get there." For others, it's flying coach across country and having the person in front of you crush your knees because they insist on putting their seat all the way back. For mothers, it might be when the kids go through three complete sets of clothing in one afternoon. For wives, it might be when your husband calls and says he'll be home by six, strolls in at seven fifteen, and wonders why you're not smiling. For fathers, it could be when you sit down to read the paper and it's been mangled by the kids and the dog before you get to it. But however widely it varies from person to person, we all have those things which push our impatience button.

A BIBLICAL PORTRAIT

Read Psalm 103:8–12

Questions Two & Three God's justice prevailed several times in the Old Testament. At the time of the Great Flood, for instance, only one family was saved from judgment. There were also wars where entire nations were wiped out. God said at certain times, "Enough is enough. Justice must prevail." But the thread that runs through the entire Old Testament is summarized in the book of Hosea, where God says, in effect, "I love My people. I called them out of Egypt. The more I called to them, the more they went from Me and offered sacrifices to idols. Yet it was I who loved them. It was I who took them into My arms, but they would not respond to Me. I led with cords and bonds of love. I lifted their yoke from them. I bent down and fed them." Then God says, "How can I give you up, My people? How can I turn you over?" I love the way Hosea 11:8 puts it: "My heart is changed within me; all my compassion is aroused."

What does this teach us about the heart of God? It is as if God is saying, "Sometimes you people push my patience to the limits. Justice begs for Me to judge you but My mercy begs for Me to extend continued grace." This battle in the heart of God didn't just happen in the Old Testament days. God is still striving with people today. God could rightly pour out judgment on unbelievers who continually rebel, go their own way, ignore Him, and live their own self-centered lives. But He doesn't! He patiently waits for unbelievers to repent.

Second Peter 3:9 says that one of the main reasons God has delayed the second coming of Jesus Christ is because He still exhibits patience. He says, "I could end the world right now, but then unchurched Harry and Mary would not be ready." He says, "It would break my heart to see unbelieving people spending an eternity in hell." You see, God has been patient with people throughout history. He's patient with people today, and He will be patient in the future as He waits for more and more people to repent.

SHARPENING THE FOCUS

Read Snapshot "When Patience Runs Out, Watch Out!" before Question 4

Question Four Deep down we all know about the high price of impatience. I've often put it this way: *"When patience runs out, watch out!"* That's when so much relational and professional damage is done. How many irresponsible marketplace decisions have been made in the heat of anger? How much spiritual damage is done when patience runs out?

When I was a kid in Michigan, fireworks were illegal. But sometimes my dad's truck drivers would bring them up from another state. We would light a bunch of firecrackers and almost all of them would go off. However, there were always a few that did not explode. Their fuses had been burned down to only about 1/16" long, but they were still live. We all knew that if we lit a match, the second the match touched the fuse, it would explode immediately. We never wanted to play around with firecrackers with short fuses because we were afraid of getting our fingers blown off.

Relationships can be like this. If we are not careful, we can be deeply hurt by people with short fuses. Also, if we are honest, we must admit that we can hurt others when we have a short fuse and let anger get the best of us. Take time in subgroups of two or three to tell your stories of the pain that has come from short fuses ignited by anger. When you pray together, be sure to lift up the broken hearts of those who have told about the damage they sustained because of relational or professional explosions they have experienced. Set aside a time of confession where each group member can confess their own times of impatience and anger to a trusted group member or to God.

Read Snapshot "God's Patience with Unbelievers" before Question 5

Question Five I pray that the Holy Spirit will overwhelm every member of your small group with the amazing reality of God's patience toward them before they became

Christians. I long for the day when people will say, "How did a holy God put up with a sinner like me all of those years? How did He put up with my thoughts, values, goals, and morality? How did He put up with the fact that I was created to worship Him, and that I refused to?" When that realization hits us, we need to all cry out, "What a patient God! What a long-suffering God! What a forbearing God!"

With that realization, the Holy Spirit helps us see the length of God's fuse toward us. He then lengthens our fuse and fills us with His supernatural patience. Slowly, quietly, deeply, genuinely He changes our whole attitude toward other people. And because we realize God has been completely patient with us, we begin wanting to be patient with other people.

Read Snapshot "God's Patience with Believers" before Question 6

Questions Six & Seven I became a Christian when I was sixteen years old, and since then, I've broken all of the Ten Commandments, either mentally or actually. My guess is that you have also. I've said immature things in front of thousands of people. I've made unwise decisions, broken a series of promises, been both slothful and overzealous, both hateful and partial to others. Over time, the Holy Spirit has shown me who I really am. As I have seen His patience towards me, I've broken down and just said, "How patient our Lord has been to put up with me all these years."

Have you been a model Christian? Are you the picture of consistency? Are you a pillar of purity, faithfulness, loyalty, and single-mindedness? Have you loved the Lord your God with all your heart, soul, mind, and strength from the moment you received Christ? The truth is that we have all tested God's patience again and again. Still, He has proven patient even in the midst of our rebellion. What amazing patience! What an example for us to follow.

As we think about God's patience, the Holy Spirit says, "Take the hint. Lighten up with others. Loosen up. Give other people the same slack that God has given you. Show a little patience and grace." God has been exceedingly patient with you. Pass it on in your relationships with others.

PUTTING YOURSELF IN THE PICTURE

Challenge group members to take time in the coming week to use part or all of this application section as an opportunity for continued growth.

SENSITIVITY

2 SAMUEL 10:1—5

INTRODUCTION

There are many Johnnys (or Janes) in our churches and probably a few in your small group. I would say that there's a little bit of Johnny in all of us. All of us have been enrolled in the school of hard knocks long enough to be able to affirm with varying degrees of passion that life is tough; it seems to get tougher and we must toughen up to survive. It is no wonder that there is a chronic lack of sensitivity in our society. The more that you are exposed to the ills of society, corruption, crime, violence, deception, accusations and indictments, the stronger your inner urge to protect yourself becomes and the harder your heart becomes. The truth is that we are all tempted to have a "Do unto others *before* they do unto us" philosophy of life. Some years ago a man expressed it to me this way, "My philosophy of life is to keep the enemy on the run." I asked him, "Who's the enemy?" He said, "Everybody!"

In the middle of a hard-hearted world we are called to live with sensitivity. In this session I am grouping together goodness, kindness, and gentleness. These three elements of the fruit of the Spirit show us that God is determined to take insensitive, hardened, toughened, callused people and transform them into sensitive, kind, courteous, gentle people. This task requires a lifelong commitment by the person of the Holy Spirit, and a lifelong commitment in the hearts and lives of followers of Christ.

THE BIG PICTURE

Take time to read this introduction with the group. There are suggestions for how this can be done in the beginning of the leader's section.

A WIDE ANGLE VIEW

Question One Every member in your group has had experiences that can cause a heart to grow hard and cold. They have all heard the conventional wisdom on the issue of tenderness. The key is to begin letting the Holy Spirit peel away the layers of hardness. A great starting point is to honestly admit that everyone has had heart-hardening experiences. Allow time for meaningful communication of some of those life experiences that have toughened the hearts of your group members.

A BIBLICAL PORTRAIT

Read 2 Samuel 10:1–5

Question Two In this seldom-noticed passage, David wanted to send his regrets to a neighboring king after the death of the king's father, so he sent emissaries to attend the funeral of the foreign dignitary. But the dead king's son, who was the new king, was counseled by his advisors to mistrust David's representatives. The new king decided to have some sport with David's personal emissaries, so he had half of their beards shaved off and cut their robes off at the waist so they were naked from the waist down.

In that time, a man's beard was a sign of masculinity. If you shaved a man's beard, you had robbed a man of his dignity. The same went for cutting off their robes. There are laws in almost every culture against disrobing people. It destroys someone's dignity to be stripped without their consent. We should remember that when our Lord was crucified, suspended between heaven and earth on a cross, He was stripped naked. That was one more way He was humiliated.

David's men were then forced to come back to Jerusalem in front of their peers, friends, and family half-shaved and naked from the waist down. When David got word of what had happened, his heart went out to these men. He hurt for them. His tender-heartedness moved him into action. While David began by expressing care and tenderness for a neighboring king who had lost his father, by the end of the passage David was extending care and concern for his own men. Although he was a warrior-king, David was also tender-hearted.

Read Snapshot "A Tender-hearted King" before Question 3

SHARPENING THE FOCUS

Read Snapshot "Empathizing Easily" before Question 4

Question Four We have all sat in front of the TV and watched what is going on in war-torn and poverty stricken parts of the world. As we watch the news, read the paper, and hear appeals for help, it is so easy to say, "Well isn't that sad.

Tough luck. It's not my problem. Boy, am I glad that didn't happen to me. What difference could I make anyway?" We can keep the walls of toughness up around our hearts and refuse to let these things impact our hearts, or we can open up and let the Holy Spirit soften us toward the hurt of others.

I remember visiting a hospital in Haiti and noticing the layers of protection around my heart. They were functioning just the way I wanted them to function. I was touched, but still protected; concerned, but still tough.

This all changed when I rounded a corner and saw a man lying in the dirt against the wall of the hospital. He had a little girl in his arms who had to be within six months of the age my daughter, Shauna, was at the time. I looked at that man and his little girl and I just knew she was not going to make it. At that moment I felt the Holy Spirit pierce through the armor around my own heart, causing me to think, "Come on, Hybels, just for a second put yourself on the ground. Lean against the stucco wall. Have no money, have no place to turn, have no hope, and have your daughter dying in your arms. Feel that." And I felt it. That is one way that the Holy Spirit begins to make a tough person tender and a callused person more compassionate.

It's not only these dramatic situations that change us, but also allowing ourselves to feel deeply in the everyday pain of life. When we hear of someone going through a divorce, we can ask, "What if that were my brother or sister? What if it was me?" When we face people who are grieving over the loss of a loved one, we can ask, "What if that were one of my parents or my child or my best friend?" When we interact with people who have lost their job, we can ask, "What if I got up tomorrow morning and had nowhere to go to work?" The key is to learn how to identify with others in their hurt and be willing to let the Holy Spirit cause our hearts to be tender and sensitive.

Imagine the difference in your home, marriage, family, marketplace, neighborhood, and church if you would really take time to step off the treadmill, cooperate with the Holy Spirit, and allow your heart to grow sensitive to the pain of others. How much more kindness would flow? How much more goodness would be exhibited? How much more gentleness would be expressed?

**Read Snapshot "Participating Personally"
before Question 5**

Questions Five & Six I remember my dad taking me, as a kid, to the Kalamazoo State Mental Hospital on Sunday afternoons. He would lead a hymn sing with about one hundred mentally retarded women. The women would hug me and often they would smell and sometimes they would drool on me. I would think, "Man, this is bad news." I would try anything to get out of going there. You see, I have always felt uncomfortable around wounded, hurting, or grieving people. I don't feel I know what to say or how to act. But guess what the Holy Spirit is doing to me? The same thing He's going to do to you. He's going to say, "Come on, tough guy. Real courage is what it takes to reach out to a stranger standing alone in the lobby of the church, visit a prisoner in jail, go into a hospital room not knowing what you're going to say, visit a nursing home, work in a food pantry, take in a homeless person, or reach out to a pregnant teenager. Real courage is allowing your heart to be tender in a world of hard-hearted people."

One of the greatest indications of the authenticity of God's work is when tough people become tender. When calloused people grow compassionate. When people get off the bench and onto the playing field. We may get some bumps and some bruises, but that is the price of living as a fully devoted follower of Christ.

Read Snapshot "Assistance in Acting Appropriately" before Question 7

Questions Seven & Eight Growing sensitive and tender will never happen naturally, but it can happen supernaturally. The Christian life is a supernatural life that started with a supernatural salvation and ends in a supernatural hereafter. And in the meantime, God, because of His great love for you, will give you the supernatural strength to become a sensitive person. Take time to tell your group members about the areas into which you feel the Holy Spirit calling you to grow sensitive and to move into action as a follower of Christ.

PUTTING YOURSELF IN THE PICTURE

Challenge group members to take time in the coming week to use part or all of this application section as an opportunity for continued growth.

FAITHFULNESS

PROVERBS 20:6–7;
REVELATION 2:8–11

INTRODUCTION

Some members of your group have been chronically unfaithful. Some have been fairly faithful. And some have been very faithful. But no matter where we are on the faithfulness scale, God loves us so much that He takes upon Himself the responsibility of transforming us into more faithful people. He has commissioned His Holy Spirit to root out unfaithfulness from our lives and to replace it with faithfulness.

We live in an "easy come, easy go" age. We dispose of diapers, razors, rules, relationships, responsibilities, and even religions. Not only do we dispose of many things, but we seem to distrust everyone. It takes a stack of legal documents for a simple business transaction these days. We hear of employment contracts and even premarriage contracts. Forget a friendly handshake sealing a deal: get it in writing, get it notarized, make multiple copies, put it in the vault, and keep a good attorney on retainer. Whatever happened to faithfulness? to trust? to commitment? to integrity? This session is focused on how we can regain this vital characteristic that God wants to grow in our lives.

THE BIG PICTURE

Take time to read this introduction with the group. There are suggestions for how this can be done in the beginning of the leader's section.

A WIDE ANGLE VIEW

Question One Allow group members to tell their stories of those who have modeled faithfulness. This will help spark hope into the discussion. It is easy to point out all of the unfaithfulness around us; however, it is critically important to hold up examples of ordinary people who have been extraordinarily faithful through the supernatural power of the Holy Spirit.

A Biblical Portrait

Read Proverbs 20:6–7; Revelation 2:8–11

Read Snapshot "What Is Faithfulness?" before Question 2

Questions Two & Three In the book of Revelation John says, "Be faithful, even to the point of death, and I will give you the crown of life" (Rev. 2:10). How faithful are we called to be? Faithful unto death. But the truth is, even if they haven't been called to be faithful to the point of death, every member of your group carries scars from times of unfaithfulness. Everyone has been hurt by the unfaithfulness of others, and everyone has hurt others, and ourselves, with our own unfaithfulness.

We've all broken promises. We've all broken commitments to family, friends, and yes, even to God. How many times have you left a Sunday church service having made a commitment to God and saying in your heart, "That's it. That particular activity or thought pattern will no longer be part of my life. I really mean it this time!" And then two days later, you're playing the same old game. Walking down the same path. We can all identify with what it means to be unfaithful.

Sharpening the Focus

Read Snapshot "Great Is Thy Faithfulness" before Question 4

Questions Four & Five King David was involved in a lot of hair-raising adventures early in his life. If you study the psalms David wrote near the end of his life, you will notice that one of the most identifiable themes in his writings is God's faithfulness and mercy. Psalm 89:1 reflects this assurance of God's faithfulness.

The people in the church where I grew up in were convinced, over many years, of God's great faithfulness. They had witnessed answers to hundreds of prayers over the course of their Christian lives. They had experienced daring rescues by God during times of trouble. They had received unexpected blessings from God's hand. They had seen the fulfillment of each and all of God's promises over time. They *had* to sing because they were just like King David—they had seen the faithfulness of God, and they had to tell others!

Over time, the Holy Spirit is going to convince you of the depth of God's faithfulness. As that realization is registered in your heart, the Holy Spirit will turn to you and say, "Take the hint. God is faithful to you. Now you be faithful to others. Be as faithful as your Father is to you." And then He will say, "I'll help you do it. When you don't have strength, I'll give you the supernatural power that you could never have on your own. Depend on me and watch what I can do in your life."

Read Snapshot "As Good As Our Word" before Question 6

Questions Six & Seven Over time, as the Holy Spirit gives you that additional realization of how faithful God is, can you guess what's going to happen? You will discover every area of your life changing in your desire to be faithful.

You're going to find yourself having the desire to be more faithful to your spouse. As you grow in your Christian life, faithfulness to your spouse will become a more natural response, even with all of the temptations and distractions around you. You're going to find yourself speaking only the truth to your spouse and consistently keeping your word.

God will also challenge you to be a man or a woman of your word to your children. Your children will remember every time you break a promise and fail to do what you say. They will also remember the times you keep your word and follow through on your promises.

Faithfulness will also have applications in the marketplace. "I'll have it for you by Monday. I'll get on it right away. I'll see to it personally. The check is in the mail." You can no longer say one thing and do another. You need to be as good as your word and faithful before God and others.

God has always dealt truthfully with you. He has never told you a lie. He isn't going to today, and He never will in the future. He says, "If you trust Me, I'll forgive your sins. If you trust Me, I'll work in your life." He says, "If you trust Me, I'll take you home to heaven." What we need to do is deal truthfully with God. Don't tell Him that you love Him on Sunday if you're going to curse Him on Monday. Don't make a promise that you're going to obey Him when you know you won't. Don't tell Him that you're going to go His way and carry out His calling and advance His purposes when you're making preparations to go your own way.

God has been faithful to you. Be faithful to Him and show His faithfulness to others. How will you do this? With the supernatural power of the Holy Spirit filling your life. There is no other way.

PUTTING YOURSELF IN THE PICTURE

Challenge group members to take time in the coming week to use part or all of this application section as an opportunity for continued growth.

ADDITIONAL WILLOW CREEK RESOURCES

Small Group Resources

Coaching Life-Changing Small Group Leaders, by Bill Donahue and Greg Bowman
The Complete Book of Questions, by Garry Poole
The Connecting Church, by Randy Frazee
Leading Life-Changing Small Groups, by Bill Donahue and the Willow Creek Team
The Seven Deadly Sins of Small Group Ministry, by Bill Donahue and Russ Robinson
Walking the Small Group Tightrope, by Bill Donahue and Russ Robinson

Evangelism Resources

Becoming a Contagious Christian (book), by Bill Hybels and Mark Mittelberg
The Case for a Creator, by Lee Strobel
The Case for Christ, by Lee Strobel
The Case for Faith, by Lee Strobel
Seeker Small Groups, by Garry Poole
The Three Habits of Highly Contagious Christians, by Garry Poole

Spiritual Gifts and Ministry

Network Revised (training course), by Bruce Bugbee and Don Cousins
The Volunteer Revolution, by Bill Hybels
What You Do Best in the Body of Christ—Revised, by Bruce Bugbee

Marriage and Parenting

Fit to Be Tied, by Bill and Lynne Hybels
Surviving a Spiritual Mismatch in Marriage, by Lee and Leslie Strobel

Ministry Resources

An Hour on Sunday, by Nancy Beach
Building a Church of Small Groups, by Bill Donahue and Russ Robinson
The Heart of the Artist, by Rory Noland
Making Your Children's Ministry the Best Hour of Every Kid's Week, by Sue Miller and
    David Staal
Thriving as an Artist in the Church, by Rory Noland

Curriculum

An Ordinary Day with Jesus, by John Ortberg and Ruth Haley Barton
Becoming a Contagious Christian (kit), by Mark Mittelberg, Lee Strobel, and Bill Hybels
Good Sense Budget Course, by Dick Towner, John Tofilon, and the Willow Creek Team
If You Want to Walk on Water, You've Got to Get Out of the Boat, by John Ortberg with
    Stephen and Amanda Sorenson
The Life You've Always Wanted, by John Ortberg with Stephen and Amanda Sorenson
The Old Testament Challenge, by John Ortberg with Kevin and Sherry Harney, Mindy
    Caliguire, and Judson Poling

Willow Creek Association

Vision, Training, Resources for Prevailing Churches

This resource was created to serve you and to help you build a local church that prevails. It is just one of many ministry tools that are part of the Willow Creek Resources® line, published by the Willow Creek Association together with Zondervan.

The Willow Creek Association (WCA) was created in 1992 to serve a rapidly growing number of churches from across the denominational spectrum that are committed to helping unchurched people become fully devoted followers of Christ. Membership in the WCA now numbers over 10,500 Member Churches worldwide from more than ninety denominations.

The Willow Creek Association links like-minded Christian leaders with each other and with strategic vision, training, and resources in order to help them build prevailing churches designed to reach their redemptive potential. Here are some of the ways the WCA does that.

- **A2: Building Prevailing Acts 2 Churches—Today**—an annual two-and-a-half day event, held at Willow Creek Community Church in South Barrington, Illinois, to explore strategies for building churches that reach out to seekers and build believers, and to discover new innovations and breakthroughs from Acts 2 churches around the country.

- **The Leadership Summit**—a once a year, two-and-a-half-day conference to envision and equip Christians with leadership gifts and responsibilities. Presented live at Willow Creek as well as via satellite broadcast to over one hundred locations across North America, this event is designed to increase the leadership effectiveness of pastors, ministry staff, volunteer church leaders, and Christians in the marketplace.

- **Ministry-Specific Conferences**—throughout each year the WCA hosts a variety of conferences and training events—both at Willow Creek's main campus and offsite, across the U.S., and around the world—targeting church leaders and volunteers in ministry-specific areas such as: evangelism, small groups, preaching and teaching, the arts, children, students, women, volunteers, stewardship, raising up resources, etc.

- **Willow Creek Resources®**—provides churches with trusted and field-tested ministry resources in such areas as leadership, evangelism, spiritual formation, spiritual gifts, small groups, stewardship, student ministry, children's ministry, the use of the arts-drama, media, contemporary music—and more.

- **WCA Member Benefits**—includes substantial discounts to WCA training events, a 20 percent discount on all Willow Creek Resources®, *Defining Moments* monthly audio journal for leaders, quarterly *Willow* magazine, access to a Members-Only section on WillowNet, monthly communications, and more. Member Churches also receive special discounts and premier services through WCA's growing number of ministry partners—Select Service Providers —and save an average of $500 annually depending on the level of engagement.

For specific information about WCA conferences, resources, membership, and other ministry services contact:

Willow Creek Association
P.O. Box 3188, Barrington, IL 60011-3188
Phone: 847-570-9812, Fax: 847-765-5046
www.willowcreek.com

InterActions
small group series

Living the
Supernatural
Life

FRUIT OF
THE SPIRIT

Interactions Small Group Series

Authenticity: Being Honest with God and Others
Character: Reclaiming Six Endangered Qualities
Commitment: Developing Deeper Devotion to Christ
Community: Building Relationships within God's Family
Essential Christianity: Practical Steps for Spiritual Growth
Fruit of the Spirit: Living the Supernatural Life
Getting a Grip: Finding Balance in Your Daily Life
Jesus: Seeing Him More Clearly
Lessons on Love: Building Deeper Relationships
Living in God's Power: Finding God's Strength for Life's Challenges
Love in Action: Experiencing the Joy of Serving
Marriage: Building Real Intimacy
Meeting God: Psalms for the Highs and Lows of Life
New Identity: Discovering Who You Are in Christ
Parenting: How to Raise Spiritually Healthy Kids
Prayer: Opening Your Heart to God
Reaching Out: Sharing God's Love Naturally
The Real Deal: Discover the Rewards of Authentic Relationships
Significance: Understanding God's Purpose for Your Life
Transformation: Letting God Change You from the Inside Out

InterActions
small group series

Living the
Supernatural
Life

Fruit of
the Spirit

Bill Hybels
with Kevin and Sherry Harney

ZONDERVAN™

GRAND RAPIDS, MICHIGAN 49530 USA

WILLOW
Willow Creek Resources

We want to hear from you. Please send your comments about this
book to us in care of zreview@zondervan.com. Thank you.

ZONDERVAN™

Fruit of the Spirit
Copyright © 1998 by Willow Creek Association

Requests for information should be addressed to:

Zondervan, *Grand Rapids, Michigan 49530*

ISBN-10: 0-310-26596-7
ISBN-13: 978-0-310-26596-2

Interior design by Rick Devon and Michelle Espinoza

Printed in the United States of America

07 08 09 10 11 12 /❖ DCI/ 10 9 8 7 6 5 4